ABCDEFGHIJKLMNOPQRSTUVWXYZ

ABC

Now I Know Common Disabilities

Written by: Elsie Guerrero

978-1-732757-39-4

ABC: Now I Know Common Disabilities
Copyright © 2019 by Elsie Guerrero

Illustrated by Jasmin Mills

Elsie Publishing Co.
Washington, DC
www.elsieguerrero.com
202.670.3282

I would like to dedicate this book to all my students with special needs. They inspired me to share their story and show the world how beautiful they are inside and out.

Let's do the alphabet. This book will illustrate the most common disabilities that you would find with children in your school and your community.

Amputation is the removal of a body part caused by trauma, medical illness, or surgery.

Attention-Deficit and Hyperactivity Disorder (ADHD) is a serious condition marked by persistent inattention, hyperactivity, and sometimes impulsivity.

Autism is a condition that begins in childhood and causes problems in forming relationships, challenges with social skills, repetitive behaviors, speech and nonverbal communication.

is for
Amputation,
ADHD, and
Autism.

B is for
Blindness

Blindness is the state or condition of not being able to see because of an injury, disease, or birth condition.

C is for Cerebral Palsy

Cerebral Palsy is a motor disorder that causes difficulty in movement and posture due to the damage in the brain.

Dyslexia is a learning disability, which causes difficulty to read or interpret words, letters, and other symbols.

Down Syndrome arises from a genetic defect It disrupts the brain functions and people with Down Syndrome often have a short stature and broad facial profile.

is for
Dyslexia and
Down Syndrome

**is for
Emotional Disturbance**

Emotional Disturbance is a condition that causes difficulty in learning and expressing oneself.

8

F

is for
Fetal Alcohol Syndrome

Fetal Alcohol Syndrome is a condition that causes slower mental development and physical growth of the skull and face.

9

G is for
Global Developmental
Delay

Global Developmental Delay is when a child is behind in one or more developmental milestones and needs special help.

H

is for Hearing Impairment

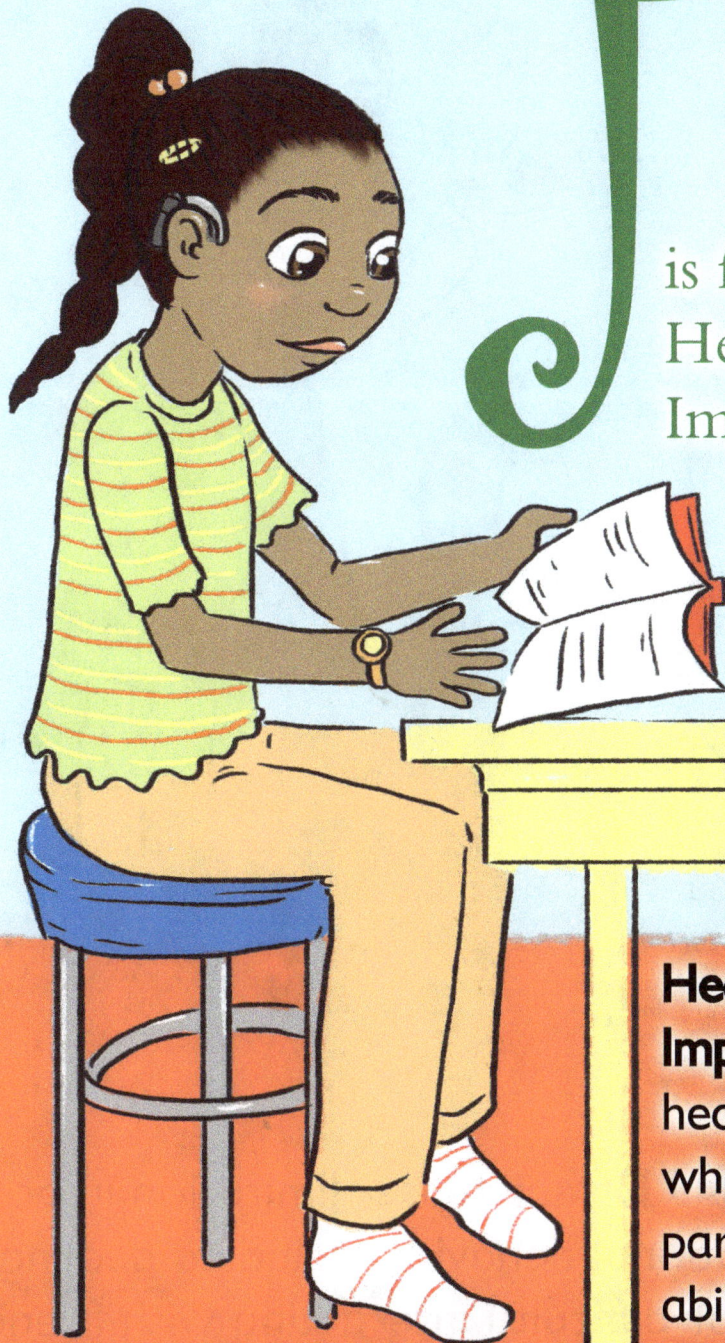

Hearing Impairment, or hearing loss, occurs when you lose part or all of your ability to hear.

11

I

is for
Intellectual Disability

Intellectual Disability is a limitation in both learning and emotional behavior, including dealing with change or difficulty interacting with friends.

Joubert syndrome is a rare genetic disorder that affects the part of the brain that controls balance and coordination.

J

is for
Joubert
Syndrome

K

is for
Kidney Disease

Kidney Disease is a short-term or long-term damage to the kidney causing the kidney not to work properly. It is a condition that may slow or block oxygen and blood to the kidneys.

14

L is for
Leukemia
Cancer

Leukemia is a type of cancer that starts in the bone marrow; the soft tissue inside most bones.

15

is for
Multiple Sclerosis

Multiple Sclerosis is a chronic disease involving damage to the sheaths of nerve cells in the brain and spinal cord.

N

Neurological Disorder is a disability that impact the brain, spine and the nerve.

is for
Obesity

Obesity is the condition of being overweight. Obesity is not a disability, but if you do not eat healthy then it can lead to other health problems.

P

is for Paralysis

Paralysis is the loss of the ability to move in part or most of the body because of illness, poison, or injury.

Q is for quick.

R is for reading.

You are quickly reading this book and learning about common types of disabilities.

S

is for Scoliosis and Sickle Cell.

Scoliosis is when the spine is curved causing an imbalance in the shoulders, hips, and legs.

Sickle Cell Anemia is a serious disease in where the red blood cells are unable to carry oxygen.

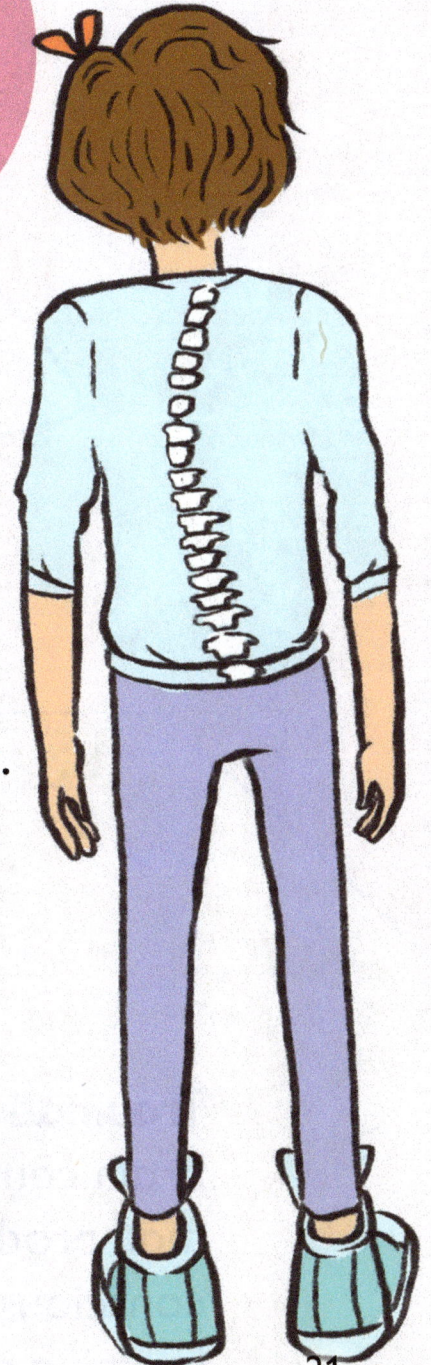

T

is for
Traumatic Brain Injury

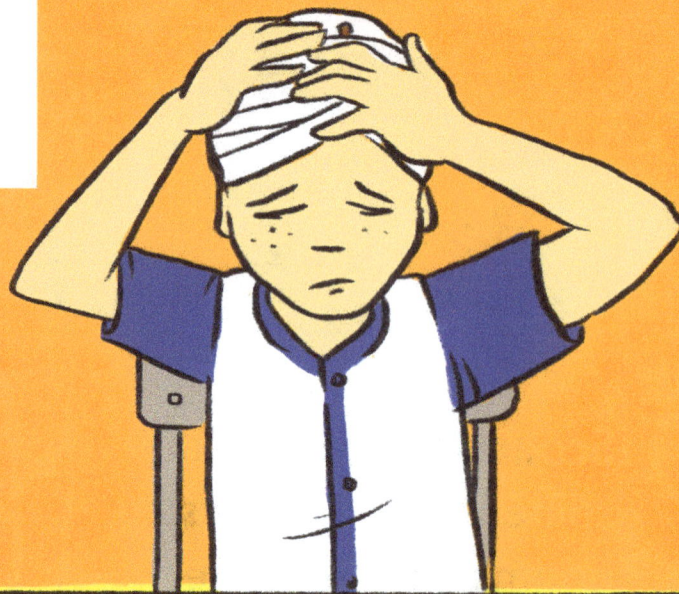

Traumatic Brain Injury is a damage to the brain caused by an external physical force that may produce a diminished or altered state of consciousness, resulting in an impairment of learning abilities or physical functioning.

22

is for Unique!

You are **UNIQUE** in your own way!

V is for
Verbal
Dyspraxia
and
Visually
Impaired.

Verbal Dyspraxia occurs when children have problem making the precise movements needed to coordinate speech, to be able to articulate words.

Visually Impaired is a decrease in ability to see. Some people with decreased ability to see do not have access to glasses or contact lenses because they cannot afford them.

is for
Wilms Tumor

Wilms Tumor is a type of cancer that starts
in the kidneys. It is the most common type of
kidney cancer in children.

X

is for X-Ray

X-Ray is a machine used to determine if someone has a disability or just to make sure that he or she is healthy.

Now you know many common disabilities. Next time read this book to a friend and teach others about the common types of disabilities.

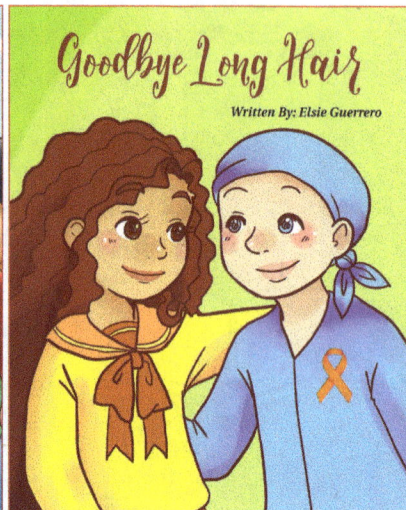

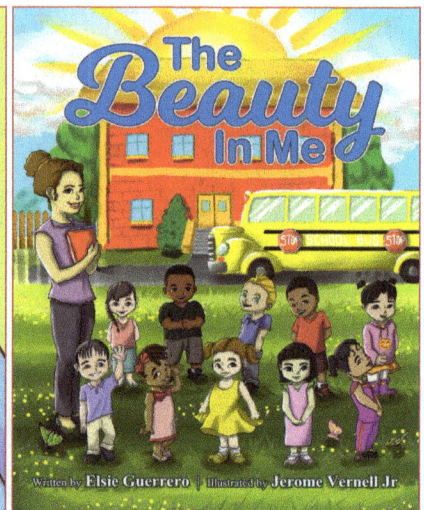